Published in the United States by Evan Ahrendt LLC
ISBN: 9781962811002

For more information or to book an event, visit our website:

www.evanahrendt.com

Paperback

Support independent publishing - please write a review.

Today is Christmas Eve,
And Santa is almost here.
Phil decorates the tree
To add some holiday cheer.

But guess who is fast asleep
In Phil's favorite chair?
That's right – it's Watson!
He loves this time of year.

And just as they both nestle in
For the night,
Watson startles awake
Thinking something's not right.

He forgot to tell Santa
What he wants most of all.
So Phil grabs his keys,
And they take off to the mall.

Everyone stands waiting,
But Santa hasn't shown.

Kids began to cry,

And parents start to moan.

Something must be wrong!
Where is Santa and his sleigh?
That's when they spot a letter
And read it right away.

Dear Watson and Phil

I hope this letter was delivered before our time runs out.
I am counting on you both! Let me tell you what it's about.

I got all turned around and am stuck at the South Pole.
My navigation system failed me, and then I lost control.

I have no way of getting home in time for Christmas Day.
Which is why I need your help, so take my other sleigh.

I need you both to deliver gifts to all who still believe.
For Christmas is a special time to give and to receive.

An extra sleigh can be found in the toy store nearest you.
Please hurry for the magic of Christmas is relying on you two!

~Santa

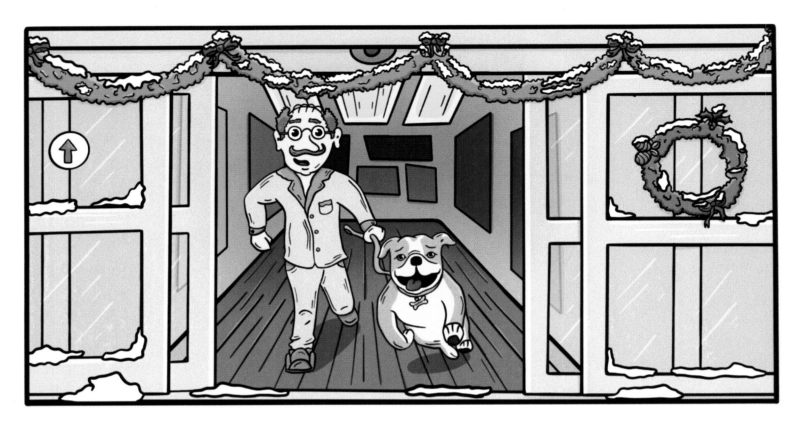

Watson gathers courage
And becomes filled with poise.
He tugs Phil out the door
And heads toward Thinker Toys.

They rush right into Thinker Toys
On this busy Christmas Eve,
Unsure of where to find his sleigh,
But know they must succeed.

Surrounded by toys and presents,
Under colorful twinkling lights,

A radiant sleigh sparkles,
Ready to take flight.

And right there on the dashboard
Of the hand crafted sled,
Is a big red button—
"SOS" is what it read.

Directions to fly Santa's Sleigh

Supplies:
- Santa Suit
- Red glowing nose & antlers
- Magic bag of gifts

Directions:
2 people required
Person 1: Put on Santa suit and deliver gifts.
Person 2: Put on magic nose and antlers and pull sleigh.

You're all set!
Take your seats and the sleigh will do the rest.

Now that they are ready
And set to take flight,
Phil starts pulling
And Watson holds on tight!

At the very first home,
They land with ease.
Watson heads to the chimney,
This might be a tight squeeze.

He squishes down the chimney
And pops out near the tree,
But is easily distracted
By the milk
and
cookies.

Phil knew this wouldn't be easy,
So many tasty treats.
Cookies are Watson's weakness,
One of his favorite sweets.

Phil quickly grabs a cookie
And helps set out the toys.

Then back up the chimney
Without making more noise.

Now back in Santa's sleigh.
Their confidence now glowing.
Watson pulls up the flight path.
"We'd better get going."

From New York and Egypt,
To Paris and Rome,
Plus so many more
Before they can head home.

The night is almost over
And soon it will be morning.
Alarm clocks start to ring,
This is the final warning.

Just three houses left,
With the sun on the rise,
They rush to finish
The Christmas surprise.

Finally at the last house,
It happens to be theirs,
They head down the chimney
And relax in their chairs.

But what is that
Peeking out from Santa's bag?
Phil reaches in,
And Watson's tail starts to wag.

Why it is what Watson
Had wished for all the while!
A crusin' new skateboard
In a hot pink style.

Attached to the skateboard,
Santa left them a letter.
"Thanks for all your hard work,
I could not have done better!"

Watson can't wait to try out
His crusin' new board,
But helping Santa save Christmas,
Was the real reward.

A present or toy
Could have never achieved
The feeling of joy
That he has received.

Watson and Phil brought the world
Holiday cheer.
Maybe Santa will let them
Fly the sleigh next year.

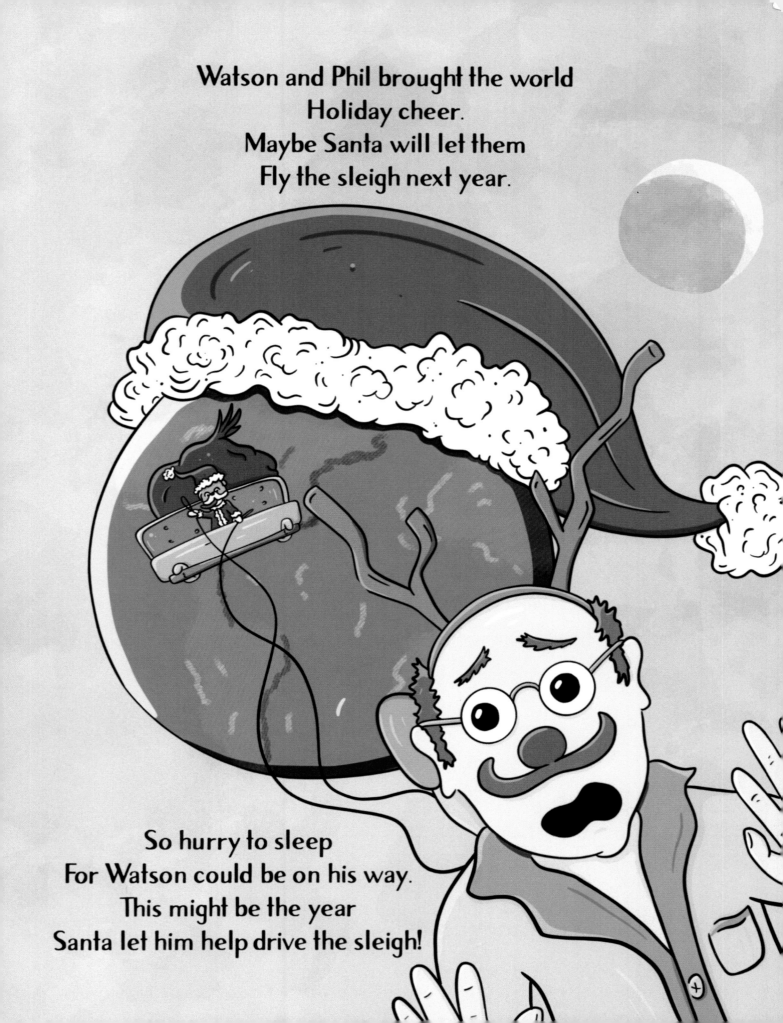

So hurry to sleep
For Watson could be on his way.
This might be the year
Santa let him help drive the sleigh!

SANTA WATSON

To my readers:
I can't believe this is my fourth book in the Watson series. When I started thinking of what I wanted to write about for my fourth book, I knew I wanted it to be a holiday book. When I began writing, the Christmas story just came to me and I went with it. I think this might be my best Watson adventure yet. I hope you enjoyed it and it becomes a Christmas favorite.

Merry Christmas,
~ Evan Ahrendt

Please help support independent publishers, like myself and leave a review on Amazon.

Made in the USA
Monee, IL
24 October 2023

44837535R00024